NATIONS IN CONFLICT
CUBA

by CHRIS HUGHES

BLACKBIRCH®
PRESS

San Diego • Detroit • New York • San Francisco • Cleveland • New Haven, Conn. • Waterville, Maine • London • Munich

For more information, contact
The Gale Group, Inc.
27500 Drake Rd.
Farmington Hills, MI 48331-3535
Or you can visit our Internet site at http://www.gale.com

Photo credits: cover, pages 6-7, 8, 9, 12, 19, 21, 23, 27, 29, 31, 32, 40, 41, 42 © CORBIS; page 5 (map) © Amy Stirnkorb Design; page 4 © Blackbirch Archive; pages 10-11 © Art Resource; page 15 © PhotoDisc; page 17 © Library of Congress; pages 24, 34, 43 © AP Wide World; pages 36, 39 © AFP

LIBRARY OF CONGRESS CATALOGING-IN-PUBLICATION DATA

Hughes, Christopher (Christopher A.), 1968-
  Cuba / by Chris Hughes.
    p. cm. — (Nations in conflict)
Includes bibliographical references and index.
  ISBN 1-41030-079-X (hardback : alk. paper)
  1. Cuba—History—Juvenile literature. 2. Revolutions—Cuba—History.
3. Cuba—Relations—United States—Juvenile literature. 4. United
States—Relations—Cuba—Juvenile literature. I. Title. II. Series.

F1776 .H84 2004
972.91—dc21   2002013547

CONTENTS

Island of Turmoil

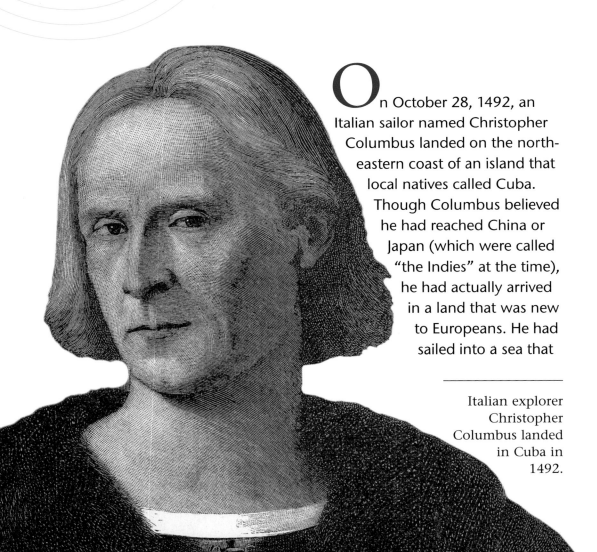

On October 28, 1492, an Italian sailor named Christopher Columbus landed on the northeastern coast of an island that local natives called Cuba. Though Columbus believed he had reached China or Japan (which were called "the Indies" at the time), he had actually arrived in a land that was new to Europeans. He had sailed into a sea that

Italian explorer Christopher Columbus landed in Cuba in 1492.

Gulf of Mexico

Florida

BAHAMAS

Key West

★Havana

CUBA

Guantanamo

Cayman Islands

Caribbean Sea

JAMAICA

would eventually be called the Caribbean, and over the course of four journeys, he explored Caribbean islands and parts of Central and South America. Columbus claimed all these lands for Spain. Neither Europe nor any of the lands in the so-called "New World," including Cuba, would ever be the same.

Ever since Columbus's arrival, Cuba has been populated by a mix of natives, Europeans, and Africans, each group with its own culture, language, and beliefs. The resulting blend of goals and ideas led to conflict and violence at times, especially during the nineteenth century.

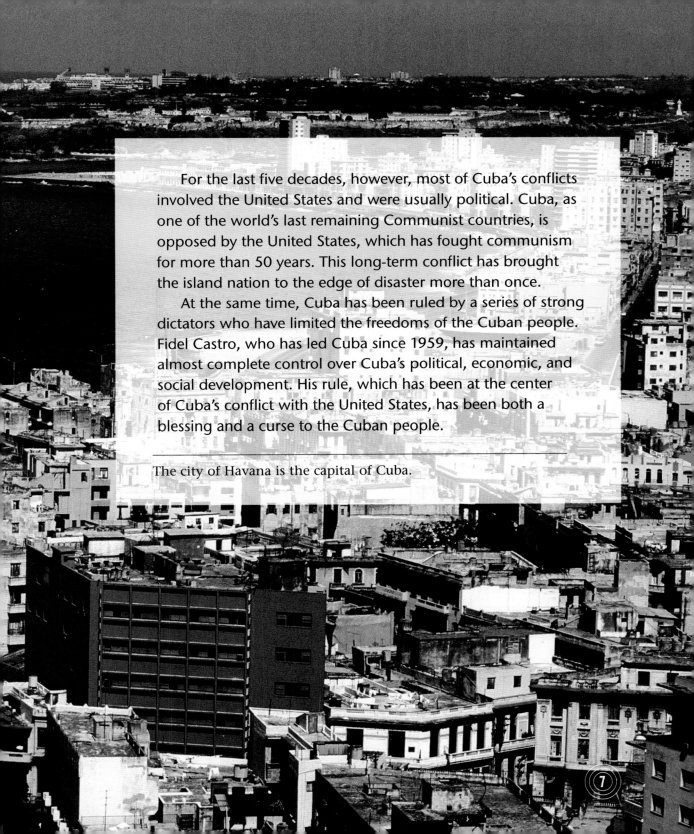

For the last five decades, however, most of Cuba's conflicts involved the United States and were usually political. Cuba, as one of the world's last remaining Communist countries, is opposed by the United States, which has fought communism for more than 50 years. This long-term conflict has brought the island nation to the edge of disaster more than once.

At the same time, Cuba has been ruled by a series of strong dictators who have limited the freedoms of the Cuban people. Fidel Castro, who has led Cuba since 1959, has maintained almost complete control over Cuba's political, economic, and social development. His rule, which has been at the center of Cuba's conflict with the United States, has been both a blessing and a curse to the Cuban people.

The city of Havana is the capital of Cuba.

CHAPTER ONE

Place, People, Past

Cuba consists of one main island that is about the size of Pennsylvania, and a number of smaller islands that are mostly uninhabited. The main island includes Havana, Cuba's capital and largest city. Mountains cover about one-quarter of Cuba, but most of the island is fertile flatland that is ideal for grazing cattle and farming.

Cuba's subtropical climate is mild. In the summer, Havana has an average high temperature of about 88°F, and in the winter, the average high is about 78°F. Like other Caribbean islands, Cuba faces the threat of both earthquakes and hurricanes. With strong winds, driving rain, and huge waves, hurricanes can destroy buildings, farms, and even entire towns.

The Spanish in Cuba

When Columbus first arrived, he found Cuba pleasant and attractive. In fact, he called it "the most beautiful land that

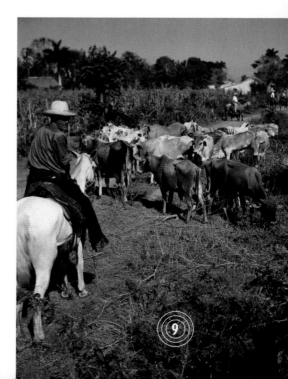

Left: Cuba's climate is ideal for growing tobacco.

Right: The island's fertile land is also well suited for raising cattle (right).

human eyes have ever seen."[1] He referred to the natives of Cuba and the other lands he visited as Indians, because he thought he had reached the Indies.

Spain's goal was to explore and conquer the New World. The Spanish believed the Americas were filled with gold and other precious metals, and they hoped to find wealth as they spread Christianity and brought the natives under their control. The Spanish chased rumors of gold throughout the Caribbean, and it was not until 1511 that they returned to Cuba. That year, Diego Velásquez sailed with 300 soldiers from the Spanish base on the nearby island of Hispaniola to conquer Cuba. This was accomplished without much difficulty, and the Spanish enslaved many natives.

The Spanish found little gold on Cuba, though there was some copper. The Indians were put to work under harsh conditions. Some mined copper and others turned the land into cattle ranches, and later, sugarcane, coffee, and tobacco plantations. Eventually, most slaves in Cuba worked on sugar plantations. Many Indians died from overwork and brutal treatment; many more died from diseases the Spanish brought, to which the Indians had no immunity. More than 100,000 Indians lived on Cuba when Columbus first arrived. By the mid-1500s, fewer than 5,000 survived.

When Christopher Columbus first arrived in Cuba, more than 100,000 Indians lived there.

As the native population fell, the Spanish imported slaves from Africa, and this slave labor allowed the Spanish to grow still more sugarcane. Soon, Cuba was one of the world's leading producers of sugar, and the mostly African slaves made up more than 35 percent of the population.

Over time, the European, Indian, and African populations mixed. This created a new Cuban culture with music, customs, and religion that blended elements from all three. This changing culture helped create a new social order. Spaniards ran the island, but Cubans (usually of Spanish descent) owned many of the plantations. The slaves remained the lowest class, without rights or privileges.

Revolts in the New World

In the 1700s and early 1800s, revolutions swept through many European-held lands in the Americas. By 1824, Spain had lost control of all its American colonies except Cuba and Puerto Rico. Many of the revolts were led by Europeans born in the Americas who no longer wanted to live under European control. In Haiti, African slaves led a revolution against Europeans.

In Cuba, local Spanish officials and wealthy landowners feared they might lose their positions—or their lives—in a slave revolt. Spain, meanwhile, feared losing the last of its possessions in the Americas. To keep Cuban landowners

Poet José Martí led a rebellion against Spain in 1895.

loyal to Spanish rule, Spain allowed them to expand their trade—for the first time, Cuban farmers were allowed to trade directly with nations other than Spain. Much of this profitable new trade was with the United States. In turn, the Cuban upper class backed the Spanish government against independence movements and several attempted slave revolts in the 1830s.

Cuba's Revolt Begins

The new trade with the United States offered Cubans a chance for wealth without Spain's high taxes. This led some Cubans to want independence, while others wanted American statehood. By the mid-1800s, labor-saving advances in sugar production had made slavery less necessary in Cuba. Cubans who sought independence from Spain were willing to consider an end to slavery if the freed slaves would, in return, support a revolution.

In 1868, a landowner named Carlos Manuel de Céspedes freed his slaves and called on Cubans to follow him in a revolt against Spain. Many Cubans responded, and Spain had to send thousands of troops to stop them. After ten years of fighting, the Spanish military defeated the rebels. In 1880, Spain finally abolished slavery in Cuba. Then, in 1895, a new rebellion against Spain began, this one led by a poet named José Martí.

Martí had spent time in the United States, and he feared that the nation would try to annex, or add, Cuba as a new state. "I have lived in the monster and I know it,"[2] he wrote of the United States in 1895. Martí wanted Cuba to be an independent nation, where people of all races could live peacefully. Though Martí himself was killed in his first battle in 1895, the revolution continued.

As Martí had predicted, the United States grew more interested in Cuba. In 1881, U.S. secretary of state James Blaine had written, "If ever ceasing to be Spanish, Cuba must necessarily become American."[3] The sugar trade had created many business ties between Cuba and the United States. As Martí's revolution continued, many Americans wanted the United States to help the Cubans fight against Spanish control. Some Americans hoped that a free Cuba would bring more trade to the United States, some wanted to annex Cuba, and others hoped to free a neighboring nation from European control.

The Spanish-American War

In 1898, a battleship called the *Maine*, sent to Havana to help protect U.S. possessions in Cuba, mysteriously exploded, and 266 sailors and marines were killed. American newspapers immediately declared that the incident was an attack by Spain. In fact, it has never been proven what caused the explosion.

Regardless of the true cause, Americans blamed Spain. "Remember the *Maine*!" became an American battle cry. The United States declared war on Spain on April 25, 1898. At the same time, Congress stated that the United States would not take over Cuba if Spain were defeated. Many Cuban revolutionaries welcomed the U.S. involvement, since their own fighting had achieved little in three years.

Spain was in no condition to fight both the Cuban revolutionaries and the resources of the United States. In December 1898, Spain and the United States signed a peace agreement that gave Cuba its freedom. At the time of the treaty, the quality of life in Cuba was poor. Education was often available only to upper-class children, and disease, hunger, and poverty were widespread. The revolutions had caused Spain to cut back Cuba's trade, and much valuable farmland had been destroyed by war. Different areas were controlled by local revolutionary leaders, and it was unclear who would rule the country when Spain withdrew.

The United States signed an agreement with Spain to grant independence to Cuba in 1898.

CUBA & THE YELLOW PRESS

William Randolph Hearst and Joseph Pulitzer were newspaper publishers who competed fiercely with each other for readers and advertisers. Each tried to be the first to print any major story, and each constantly looked for ways to boost sales of their papers. In 1895, Pulitzer's *New York World* ran America's first regular feature comic strip, and Hearst's *New York Journal* began to run its own comics the next year. Pulitzer's first strip was called "Yellow Kid," and other papers began to refer to the *World* and the *Journal* as the "yellow press."

In 1898, Hearst and Pulitzer both saw a chance to take advantage of Cuba's ongoing revolution against Spain. The two publishers recognized that there were many people in America who might favor the expansion of America's territory, especially if the United States could do so as part of a "noble cause." The Cubans' fight for freedom from Spain seemed to be that cause. In 1898, Hearst published a private letter from the Spanish minister to the United States, which contained insults about U.S. president William McKinley. The letter had been stolen by a Cuban rebel. This made more Americans angry with Spain and willing to help Cuba.

Hearst and Pulitzer sent journalists and artists to Cuba to report on how the Spanish treated Cubans. Some of what they reported was exaggerated, and some was completely false. In some cases, reporters filed stories without ever going to Cuba. According to one often-repeated story, an artist Hearst had sent to Cuba in 1897 to cover the war wrote to the publisher and asked to come home because there was no war. Hearst replied, "Please remain. You furnish the pictures, I'll furnish the war." A few months later, the *Maine* exploded. The "yellow journalism" of Hearst and Pulitzer helped convince the American people that Spain was behind the explosion, and the United States went to war with Spain.

William Randolph Hearst used his newspaper to help fuel the war between Spain and the United States.

The United States in Cuba

Although the United States had promised not to annex Cuba, it put its own military governor in charge and began a series of projects to rebuild the nation. Education, public health, and job-training programs were started or improved. The United States also wrote and approved Cuba's new constitution, which called for the country's first democratic government. Although these changes benefited many Cubans, many also remembered the warnings of José Martí. They wondered if the United States would ever let Cuba be truly independent.

The United States remained involved in Cuba over the next several decades, even after the military governor was replaced by an elected president and a prime minister chosen by the legislature in 1902. The Platt Amendment, passed by the U.S. Congress in 1901, gave the United States the right to intervene in Cuba at any time to "protect" the island. In 1903, an American military base was built at Guantanamo Bay on Cuba's eastern shore, and Cuba gave the United States permanent rights to the base. Three times between 1906 and 1917, U.S. troops were sent to establish order when uprisings threatened the elected governments. Cuban leaders were often accused of corruption, and many Cubans believed their presidents were paid and controlled by the United States.

American influence in Cuba went beyond military action, though. During the 1920s, U.S. companies bought much of the island's best farmland. With so many military and economic connections, Havana became a popular vacation spot for Americans. The influx of American dollars also helped tie Cuba and its leaders to the United States, and created even more resentment for the Platt Amendment and U.S. control over Cuba.

Fulgencio Batista used the military to make himself dictator of Cuba in 1952.

ERNESTO "CHE" GUEVARA

Born in Argentina in 1928, Ernesto "Che" Guevara studied medicine and earned his medical degree in 1953. The next year, while he traveled in Guatemala, he saw United States–backed forces overthrow the Socialist government of Jacobo Arbenz Guzmán. Guevara thought the U.S. action was unjust, and it helped convince him to take a stand against the capitalist democracy of the United States. Guevara became a committed Communist.

In 1956, Guevara met Fidel Castro, who was in exile in Mexico. Guevara decided to join Castro's struggle, and later that year, they returned to Cuba to launch a new revolution against dictator Fulgencio Batista. Guevara became an expert in guerrilla warfare. When Batista was defeated in 1959, Castro put Guevara in charge of the trials of Batista's former security force. Guevara also helped organize Cuba's new military and Castro's own security forces.

Through 1959 and into 1960, Guevara convinced Castro to embrace communism. Guevara was behind much of the nationalization and agricultural reform that led the United States to oppose Castro. Guevara also helped Castro develop ties with the Soviet Union. Guevara traveled across the world as Castro's personal ambassador and built ties with Communist leaders in Africa, Europe, and Asia. By 1965, however, Guevara began to feel that the Soviet Union was only using Cuba and other nations for its own purposes. He left Cuba to spread his own brand of revolution and guerrilla warfare. In 1966, he was captured as he tried to launch a revolution in Bolivia. On October 9, 1967, Guevara was executed.

In Cuba, Guevara has remained a national hero. During the Cold War, Cuban soldiers who returned from Communist struggles in other nations were awarded a medal for following "El Camino de Che" or "The Path of Che." Even today, Cuban children are encouraged to "be like Che" by devoting their lives to the service of Cuba, Castro, and communism.

Communist revolutionary Ernesto "Che" Guevara is considered a national hero in Cuba.

Batista Comes to Power

In 1933, an army sergeant named Fulgencio Batista organized a successful revolution against Cuba's corrupt government. Although Batista did not immediately take control of the government, for most of the next 20 years, he was the most powerful figure in Cuba, and he put people he controlled in office. Batista himself was elected president in 1940 and served until 1944. He ran for reelection in 1952, but when his defeat appeared certain, he used the military to take over Cuba and make himself dictator.

During his years in power, Batista convinced the United States to cancel the Platt Amendment, but he allowed the Americans to keep their naval base at Guantanamo Bay. Over time, Batista's violent use of government forces against any opposition made him unpopular both at home and in the United States. By the late 1950s, U.S. president Dwight D. Eisenhower called Batista a "self-enriching and corrupt dictator."[4]

Castro's Revolution

In 1953, a rebellion against Batista began, led in part by a young lawyer named Fidel Castro. The son of a prosperous landowner, Castro had often spoken out against American influence in Cuba. Castro had been running for a seat in Cuba's congress when Batista overthrew the government, and he tried to sue Batista for violating Cuba's constitution. When the courts refused to hear his claim in 1953, Castro led an attack on the Moncada army barracks in Santiago.

Castro and his supporters, including his brother Raúl, were captured, but in 1955, they were released and exiled to Mexico. In 1956, Castro returned to Cuba and continued the revolution with support from an

President Dwight D. Eisenhower called Cuba's president Fulgencio Batista a "corrupt dictator."

Argentinean revolutionary named Ernesto "Che" Guevara. Although they were almost defeated again, Castro and Guevara were able to hide in the mountains and build up their forces. After more than a year of guerrilla warfare against Batista's forces, Castro won. On December 31, 1958, Batista fled Cuba. In February, Castro named himself prime minister. Castro has remained the only real power in Cuba since 1959.

CHAPTER TWO

Political Turmoil

Castro's fight against Batista made him a hero to many of Cuba's poor. Under Batista, Cuba had been filled with crime and corruption. Although high sugar prices still brought money into the country, most of it went to the small upper class. Basic necessities such as health care and education were not generally available to Cuba's poor, but the wealthy lived in luxury. Many poor Cubans strongly resented the United States because American businesses had so much property and influence in Cuba. The poor had no way to challenge Batista, however. Any opposition to his rule was usually put down with violence.

Castro convinced the poor that they would be better off with him in charge than they were under Batista. Cuba's wealthy people, however, watched him with fear. American companies were also concerned; they feared Castro would take away the protections they had enjoyed under Batista. They knew that Castro was influenced by Che Guevara, a Communist who wanted to put all industry under government control.

Nationalization of Industry

Almost immediately, Castro began to nationalize industries—take them away from private owners and turn them over to the government.

Fidel Castro, pictured here in 1977, came to power in Cuba in 1959.

This allowed him to lower prices for average citizens, but it was a huge loss to business owners. Many wealthy Cubans fled to the United States and took much of their money with them. American companies also lost property. By the middle of 1960, Castro had ordered all U.S. businesses in Cuba to be nationalized.

The United States condemned Castro's actions. The nationalization meant a huge loss of money and land for U.S. companies and stockholders. In response, the United States boycotted Cuban sugar. This embargo soon expanded to include almost all Cuban products, and prohibited trade between the two nations. For help, Cuba turned to the Soviet Union, which agreed to pay high prices for Cuban sugar. This helped the Cuban economy make up for losses caused by the American embargo.

Between 1945 and 1991, during the Cold War, the United States and the Soviet Union opposed each other at every opportunity. The capitalist democracy of the United States stood against the Communist Soviet Union, and each side tried to spread its influence to other nations. Americans saw Cuba's growing relationship with the Soviet Union as a major threat, since the U.S. border was only 90 miles from Cuba. It was a threat that the United States decided to face quickly.

The Bay of Pigs Invasion

In 1960, the United States began to train refugees from Cuba to invade their homeland and overthrow Castro. In April 1961, about 1,400 armed refugees landed at the Bay of Pigs on Cuba's southern coast. Although the rebels received training and weapons from the United States, President John F. Kennedy did not allow American troops to take part. The planners of the mission hoped the Cuban people would rise up against Castro when the invasion began, but they underestimated

Castro's popularity among the poor. They also failed to contact anyone in Cuba who might have opposed Castro, and the lack of direct U.S. military support left the invaders unprotected on the beach. In less than three days, almost all of the rebels were captured or killed.

It was one of the lowest points in U.S. international relations. Kennedy admitted that the United States had backed the rebels, and he had to give Cuba more than $50 million worth of medicine and supplies to free some of the imprisoned invaders. Castro declared in a 1961 speech, "Throughout the whole world there are demonstrations in support of us and against the United States. They [U.S. leaders] are surprised because in less than 72 hours we have destroyed the invasion which was prepared by the brains of the

President John F. Kennedy admitted that the United States had backed the rebels in the 1960 Bay of Pigs invasion.

Pentagon with all the tactics and preparations of a war."[5] A week after the invasion, Castro publicly confirmed that he was a Communist and a strong supporter of the Soviet Union. In response, the United States extended its embargo to all Cuban goods and trade until Cuba's government changed.

The Cuban Missile Crisis

In October 1962, an American spy plane took photographs of nuclear missile sites under construction in Cuba. Fearing another U.S. invasion, Castro had asked for protection from the Soviets, who, in response, had provided the missile sites. The United States immediately saw the missiles as a threat to American safety. After he and his advisors explored several options—including an invasion of Cuba and an air strike on the missile bases—Kennedy decided to "quarantine" Cuba. This meant that the U.S. Navy would stop and examine all ships that attempted to bring goods to Cuba. Any vessel with military equipment would not be allowed to proceed.

This was a dangerous move. If the navy stopped and searched a Soviet ship on the open sea, it would be considered an act of war. In a letter to Castro, Soviet leader Nikita Khrushchev wrote, "We on our part will do everything to stabilize the situation in Cuba, to defend Cuba from invasion."[6] After 13 tense days during which the world wondered if a nuclear war was about to begin, the United States and the Soviet Union came to an agreement. The Soviets would remove their missiles from Cuba; in return, the United States would agree not to invade Cuba and would remove its own missiles from Turkey, near the Soviet border. This event, which came to be known as the Cuban Missile Crisis, brought Cuba and the Soviets even closer together.

Although the embargo was the most visible method the United States

Fidel Castro (left) visited Soviet leader Nikita Khrushchev (right) in 1963.

used to oppose Castro, it was not the only one. The United States pressured other nations to join the embargo by offering them better trade deals or aid packages, or by withholding aid if they traded with Cuba. American leaders also tried more direct tactics. A 1967 CIA report described a number of assassination plots that the United States had planned or attempted against Castro. For example, a poisoned milkshake was left on his desk, he received an exploding cigar, and a paid assassin was hired.

Castro Transforms Cuba

Within Cuba, Castro began to transform society. He freed people from social and economic restrictions based on race, class, sex, or occupation. For the first time, women were allowed to work in all fields of business and government. When Castro came to power, Cuba was a rural, agricultural nation. Castro brought in industry and technology, and more people began to move to cities and to more stable jobs.

Education was another matter Castro addressed. In 1959, most Cubans could not read, and few children had access to schools. Castro developed a free education system designed to reach all of Cuba's children. Today, education is required for all children through age 14, and 96 percent of Cubans can read.

Castro also created a health-care system to give high-quality service to all Cubans at no cost. This program dramatically improved Cuba's health care. More Cuban children survive infancy and live longer lives than in almost any other nation in Central or South America or the Caribbean. In addition, major programs of health education, treatments, and shots helped eliminate or control many diseases.

Despite these improvements, though, the basic rights of most Cubans remained at least as limited under Castro as they had been under Batista. Castro had complete control over Cuban politics. It was risky to challenge him. Prisons filled with people who dared to speak out against him, and his opponents faced torture or death. In some cases, Castro exiled his enemies from Cuba and took their property.

Religion was another area in which Cubans lost their freedom. Most were members of the Roman Catholic Church, and Castro banned organized religion. He closed Catholic churches and schools and exiled or jailed foreign priests. Any religious service had to be held in secret.

Fidel Castro developed a free education system in Cuba and required that all children attend school.

Castro was a dictator who kept direct control over the military and news agencies. For many years, he refused to name a successor or second-in-command because he did not want anyone to be in a position to challenge his power. Not until 2001 did Castro choose his younger brother Raúl as his successor.

Communist Cuba

Castro soon made Cuba a major contributor to the attempt to spread communism. Through the 1970s and 1980s, Cuban troops fought in many countries in Asia, Africa, and Latin America against capitalist or pro–United States forces. Cuban advisors in those countries worked to promote communism and develop health care, education, and economic programs like those in Cuba. This brought Cuba into conflict with many

Cubans had to stand in line for oranges in Havana during the food crises of the early 1990s.

non-Communist governments, especially in Latin America. They viewed Castro as a threat to their safety, and many chose to join the U.S. embargo against Cuban trade.

Eventually, though, Cuba lost its biggest supporter. In the mid-1980s, the Soviet Union faced a major economic crisis. Cuba had long received a huge amount of Soviet money, food, and supplies, but by 1990, continued economic problems forced Soviet leaders to end that support. The next year, the Soviet Union collapsed. Cuba was left without a strong ally for the first time since Castro took over in 1959.

Until the 1990s, the U.S. embargo had barely affected Cuba because the Soviets had been able to meet Cuba's trade needs. After the fall of the Soviet Union, however, the Cuban economy began to collapse. Production dropped more than 30 percent in the three years after Soviet aid ended, and Cubans faced huge shortages of food and basic medical supplies. The country had become so reliant on trade with the Soviets that it had not built trade relations with other nations. Also, the Soviet Union had bought Cuban goods at very high prices to support the Cuban economy. No other nation was willing to match those prices.

After the Fall of the Soviet Union

The loss of Soviet funding, combined with the U.S. embargo, created hardships for Cuba's medical program. Cuba started a two-tiered health-care system. The top level, for government officials and tourists, remained excellent; the second level, for most of Cuba's population, struggled to provide decent care. This resulted in an increase in the spread of infectious diseases, which had been under control only a decade earlier.

Access to food was limited for most Cubans. The government issued ration cards that determined what items Cubans could buy. Even Cuban-made products such as sugar were rationed, because Cuba sold most of them to other nations. Non-rationed food was accessible only to government officials and tourists. Beginning in 1994, Cuban farmers were allowed to sell extra crops in markets. (Before this, the government had controlled all food production and sales.) This brought more fresh produce to the cities, but still, for most Cubans, all but the most basic foods were either not available or not affordable.

Cuba began to see other changes as well. Castro loosened some aspects of the Communist system, and allowed private companies and individuals to work for profits instead of for fixed government pay. More private businesses developed, and tourism replaced sugar production as the most important industry. Castro also began to ease religious restrictions. After years of persecution, the Roman Catholic Church functioned openly again.

CHAPTER THREE

Cuba's Future

Cuba faces two major conflicts in its immediate future. The first is the ongoing U.S. embargo. In place since 1960, the embargo remains one of the main obstacles to prosperity. Without the economic or political support of the United States, Cuba has not been able to meet its demands for food, medicine, or supplies since the early 1990s. The other conflict in Cuba is the leadership of Fidel Castro, and what might happen to Cuba after his death or fall.

The embargo has become a major source of disagreement within the United States and throughout the world. In the U.S. Congress, there are Republicans and Democrats on both sides of the debate. Those who oppose the embargo believe it hurts the Cuban people, especially the poor, but does not affect Castro. Some American leaders even feel that Castro is no longer enough of a threat to be worth the trouble. Those who favor the embargo think it is the best way to remove Castro from power.

In the 1990s, income for cab drivers increased when tourism replaced sugar as Cuba's most important industry.

In 2002, former U.S. president Jimmy Carter (left) traveled to Cuba and met with Fidel Castro (right).

Arguments Against the Embargo

In May 2002, former U.S. president Jimmy Carter traveled to Cuba. There, he made speeches that called for democracy and more freedom in Cuba, but also called for an end to the embargo. The embargo "induces anger and resentment, restricts the freedoms of U.S. citizens and makes it difficult for us to exchange ideas and respect," Carter told a crowd in Havana.[7] Castro welcomed Carter's visit, which many people took as a sign that the Cuban dictator would like to improve his relations with the United States. Still, Castro has consistently said that he will never change Cuba's overall economic policy.

Other nations and international organizations have appealed for an end to the embargo. On his 1998 visit to Cuba, Pope John Paul II called for an end to the sanctions. The United Nations has consistently opposed the embargo since the 1991 fall of the Soviet Union, to no avail. In 1992, the embargo was even expanded to punish other countries through fines or trade limitations if they gave assistance to Cuba. In 1996, the embargo was tightened even further when president Bill Clinton signed the Helms-Burton Act. This law allowed U.S. companies that lost land to nationalization in Cuba to sue foreign companies that do business in Cuba. It also allowed the United States to ban executives of those companies from traveling to the United States, and fined any U.S. citizen who traveled to Cuba without U.S. government approval. The American government hoped that the Cuban people would finally rise up and remove Castro in the face of their crisis. That hope—the same hope that was behind the Bay of Pigs invasion in 1961—still has not come true.

POPE JOHN PAUL II'S VISIT TO CUBA

In 1998, a visit to Cuba by Pope John Paul II helped show Cubans and the world that Castro had softened his views on religion and the Roman Catholic Church. For many years, Castro had declared Cuba an atheist nation, or one that does not believe in God. Soon after the fall of the Soviet Union, however, Castro began to call Cuba a "secular," or nonreligious, nation instead.

Before 1959, 85 percent of Cuba's population was Roman Catholic, and even under Castro's rule, devout Catholics found ways to worship in secret. Although major Christian holidays were not observed, the people followed their religion behind closed doors. As Castro's restrictions on organized religion began to decrease, Cubans were able to worship more publicly and Catholic churches began to reopen.

The pope used his visit to speak out against many of Castro's policies, including the years of enforced atheism and the lack of freedoms. He asked Castro to free political prisoners and to allow political opponents to be heard. He also asked for more religious freedom for Cuba's Catholics.

In his speeches, the pope spoke against "uncontrolled capitalism" and specifically against the U.S. embargo, which he described as unethical and unjust because of the hardships it placed on the Cuban people. This was what Castro had hoped for when he invited the pope to visit Cuba.

Most of the pope's public appearances during his five-day visit were attended by either Fidel or Raúl Castro. For them, the cost of allowing increased religious free-dom was a small price to pay in exchange for winning a powerful ally against the U.S. embargo.

Pope John Paul II was welcomed to Cuba by Fidel Castro in 1998.

Cuba's Record on Human Rights

Recently, the United States has pointed to Cuba's record on human rights to explain why the embargo remains in place. According to the UN, human rights are those rights that are supposed to apply to all people throughout the world. These include civil and political rights,

which give people equal opportunities and a voice in their government. They also include child labor laws, rights for prisoners and people accused of crimes, and basic rights that protect people's safety. In some of these areas, Fidel Castro has developed programs such as those in health care, social equality, and education that have achieved excellent results.

Other human rights issues, particularly political rights, have not been addressed, though. The Cubans who seem not to have these rights happen to be those who oppose Castro or his government. These dissenters are sometimes exiled, but more often they are sent to jail as political prisoners. The United States and human rights organizations have claimed that

Cuba's military is a strong presence in everyday life.

Cuba tortures and abuses these political prisoners, and keeps them in jail without fair trials to determine whether they are guilty of a crime. In its 2001 report, the UN Commission on Human Rights "expressed concern at the continued violation of such human rights and fundamental

Protests against Castro are not allowed in Cuba. The man pictured was arrested for participating in this 1998 rally in Havana.

freedoms as freedom of expression, association and assembly and the rights associated with the administration of justice."[8] The commission felt that the basic rights of free speech, fair trials, and the freedom to assemble were not honored in Cuba.

It is a crime to speak out against Castro's government or against Cuba. There are also few political choices. Castro's government does not have true elections. The Cuban Communist Party, led by Castro, is the only party allowed. Even though Cubans are allowed to vote for the legislature, called the National Assembly, the only people who may run for these seats are those Castro deems acceptable. The National Assembly

Fidel Castro casts his vote for president in 2002. All political candidates must be approved by Castro before they can run for office.

then elects the president. In 1998, Fidel and his brother Raúl were reelected as president and first vice president with 100 percent of the National Assembly vote.

The Continuing Problem of Castro

Castro's presidency is at the center of Cuba's conflict with the United States. At various times, American presidents have declared that the embargo will not be lifted while Castro is in office. In May 2002, however, president George W. Bush indicated that the sanctions might be eased if Castro were still in power, as long as he opened the election process to allow political opponents to run against him in a free election.

Castro has ruled Cuba so completely since 1959 that there is no clear system in place to govern Cuba if he should die. As Castro ages, his health is a point of concern. Although Castro chose his brother Raúl to be his successor, many people feel Raúl is too weak to be an effective leader. Only five years younger than Fidel, Raúl is also old enough to make Cubans worry about his health. Although some experts believe that Raúl might open the door to better relations with the United States, others point out that he has been a committed Communist for as long as Fidel. If Raúl does not outlive Fidel, or if he is not strong enough to keep control of Cuba's government, Cuba could fall into a state of chaos as various groups try to take power.

From the U.S. point of view, any change in Cuba's leadership would probably be a positive step. Over a peri-

Raúl Castro, Fidel's brother, was elected as vice president in 1998.

od of more than 40 years, ten different American presidents have waited for the Cuban people to overthrow their dictator. Despite an armed invasion, economic isolation, and near financial ruin, the Cubans have not taken any significant action against Castro. His supporters declare that this is a sign of his popularity, while his enemies say it shows how much people fear him. The truth probably lies somewhere in the middle. Some Cubans value the changes Castro has brought to the nation, and others rightly fear his anger. In any event, it seems clear that Cuba will not achieve prosperity as long as it stands against the United States, and the United States will not reach out to a Cuba that is run by Fidel Castro.

Important Dates

1492	Christopher Columbus lands in Cuba.
1511	Spain begins to occupy Cuba actively under Diego Velásquez.
Mid-1500s	Native Cuban population falls to a few thousand; Spain heavily increases importation of African slaves.
	Havana falls to British; Cuba's trade increases, as does its number of slaves.
1868	Cuba's first war for independence, led by Carlos Manuel de Céspedes, begins.
1895	Cuba's second war for independence, led by José Martí, begins.
1898	U.S.S. *Maine* explodes in Havana Harbor; United States joins war against Spain; Cuba becomes independent from Spain.
1901	Platt Amendment gives United States right to be involved in Cuban affairs.
1903	United States gains Guantanamo Naval Base.
1933	Army sergeant Fulgencio Batista leads revolt.
1952	Batista becomes dictator of Cuba.
1953	Fidel and Raúl Castro attempt revolt against Batista; both are exiled.
1956	Fidel Castro returns to Cuba with help of Che Guevara to restart his revolution.
1959	Batista flees Cuba.
1960	Castro begins to nationalize property in Cuba; United States begins embargo of Cuba.
1961	Bay of Pigs invasion attempted by Cuban refugees trained by United States fails.
1962	Cuban Missile Crisis takes place.
1967	Che Guevara executed in Bolivia.

1991	Soviet Union falls; trade and financial support to Cuba dropped.
1992	United States passes "Cuban Democracy Act," which threatens sanctions against any nation that aids Cuba.
1996	United States passes Helms-Burton Act, which further tightens embargo.
1998	Pope John Paul II visits Cuba.
2002	Former U.S. president Jimmy Carter visits Cuba; he pushes for increased democracy and freedom and calls for end to U.S. embargo.

About the Author

Chris Hughes holds a B.A. in history from Lafayette College and an M.A. in social studies education from Lehigh University. A history teacher and school administrator, Hughes teaches both U.S. and world history and has written several books on the American Civil War and on developing nations. Hughes currently lives and works at a boarding school in Chatham, Virginia, with his wife, Farida, and their children, Jordan and Leah.

For More Information

WEBSITES

www.canfnet.org   Cuban American National Foundation website, set up by Cubans opposed to Castro (mostly living in the United States).

www.cuba.com   Official web page for Cuba; primarily travel information.

www.cubafacts.com   Information on modern and historical Cuba.

www.cubaheritage.com   Website with information on Cuban history, culture, and biographies.

www.hrw.org   Website for Human Rights Watch, an international organization based in the United States.

www.lonelyplanet.com   Travel-focused website with information on Cuban history and daily life.

www.odci.gov/cia/publications/factbook
World Factbook 2001, created by United States Central Intelligence Agency (CIA).

www.state.gov/r/pa/ei/bgn   U.S. State Department background notes on nations.

BOOKS

Cuba, by Victoria Sherrow (Twenty-first Century Books, 2001).
Cuba, by Mary Virginia Fox (Lucent Books, 1999).
The Cuban Missile Crisis, by Catherine Hester Gow (Lucent Books, 1997).
Fidel Castro: An Unauthorized Biography, by Petra Press (Heinemann Library, 2000).
José Martí: Cuban Patriot and Poet, by David Goodnough (Enslow Publishers 1996).
Remember the Maine: *The Spanish-American War Begins*, by Tim McNeese (Morgan Reynolds, 2001).

Source Quotations

1. Quoted in Yale-New Haven Teachers Institute, The Heritage of Puerto Rico and Cuba, found on-line at www.yale.edu/ynhti/curriculum/units/1989/3/89.03.02.x.html#h; accessed August 5, 2002.

2. Unfinished letter to Manuel Mercado, Dos Rios, Cuba, May 18, 1895, found on-line at web.usf.edu/~lc/MOOs/cuba/martimon.htm; accessed August 1, 2002.

3. Quoted in J. A. Sierra, The History of Cuba, found on-line at www.historyofcuba.com/history/scaw/scaw1.htm); accessed August 7, 2002.

4. Quoted in Carmelo Mesa-Lago, ed., *Revolutionary Change in Cuba* (University of Pittsburgh Press, 1971), p. 47.

5. Castro Denounces U.S. Aggression, speech delivered in Havana, April 24, 1961; text found on-line at www.lanic.utexas.edu/la/cb/cuba/castro/1961/19610423; accessed August 5, 2002.

6. Letter to Fidel Castro from Nikita Khrushchev, dated October 28, 1962; text found on-line at oll.temple.edu/hist249/course/Documents/letter_to_fidel_castro_from_niki.htm; accessed August 6, 2002.

7. Carter Urges Democracy in Cuba, reported on CNN.com on May 15, 2002; article found on-line at www.cnn.com/2002/WORLD/americas/05/14/carter.cuba/; accessed August 7, 2002.

8. Report on United Nations Commission of Human Rights, Fifty-seventh session, 2001; found on-line at www.hri.ca/uninfo/unchr2001/contents.htm; accessed August 8, 2002.

Index